Rookie
Read-About®
Science

How Things Work:
Lightbulbs

by Joanne Mattern

Content Consultant

Hal Wallace, Electricity Curator
National Museum of American History
Smithsonian Institution

Reading Consultant

Jeanne M. Clidas, Ph.D.
Reading Specialist

Children's Press®
An Imprint of Scholastic Inc.

A CIP catalog record of this book is available from the Library of Congress.
ISBN 978-0-531-21368-1 (library binding) – ISBN 978-0-531-21456-5 (pbk.)

Produced by Spooky Cheetah Press
Design by Keith Plechaty

© 2016 by Scholastic Inc.

All rights reserved. Published in 2016 by Children's Press, an imprint of Scholastic Inc.

Printed in China 62

SCHOLASTIC, CHILDREN'S PRESS, ROOKIE READ-ABOUT®, and associated logos are trademarks and/or registered trademarks of Scholastic Inc.

1 2 3 4 5 6 7 8 9 10 R 25 24 23 22 21 20 19 18 17 16

Photographs ©: cover: Nick White/Media Bakery; 3 top left: ktsimage/Thinkstock; 3 top right: Janine Lamontagne/iStockphoto; 3 bottom: Kareivis/Thinkstock; 4: Pablo77/Shutterstock, Inc.; 7: VvoeVale/iStockphoto; 11: Willis Glassgow/AP Images; 12 boy: Deyan Georgiev/Shutterstock, Inc.; 12 hanging lightbulb: Chones/Shutterstock, Inc.; 12 burned out lightbulb: Deyangeorgiev/Dreamstime; 15: North Wind Picture Archive; 16: Science and Society/Superstock, Inc.; 19 main: Bettmann/Corbis Images; 19 inset: SSPL/Science Museum/ Art Resource, NY; 20: Jamie GrillJGI/Media Bakery; 22: Kareivis/Thinkstock; 23: Andrew Cribb/iStockphoto; 24: beboy/Shutterstock, Inc.; 26-27 neon frames: Gunnar Pippel/Shutterstock, Inc.; 26 top: Mary Evans Picture Library/Alamy Images; 26 center: SSPL/Science Museum/ Art Resource, NY; 26 bottom: Bettmann/Corbis Images; 27 top: Anthony Aneese Totah Jr/Dreamstime; 27 center left: Oleksiy Mark/Shutterstock, Inc.; 27 center right: Janine Lamontagne/iStockphoto; 27 bottom: Bizipix/Dreamstime; 30: Stocktrek Images/Getty Images; 31 top: VvoeVale/iStockphoto; 31 center top: Science and Society/Superstock, Inc.; 31 center bottom: ArturNyk/Thinkstock; 31 bottom: ktsimage/Thinkstock.

Illustrations by Jeffrey Chandler/Art Gecko Studios!

Table of Contents

Lighting Up the Dark

The colorful lights of a carnival light up the night. A reading lamp glows in the dark. We have gotten very used to these things. But have you ever wondered why it is so easy for us to light up our world?

It starts with **electricity**. Plug in a lamp. Electricity flows in through the wire.

Just providing electricity is not enough, though. You need a lightbulb, too! But how does the lightbulb work?

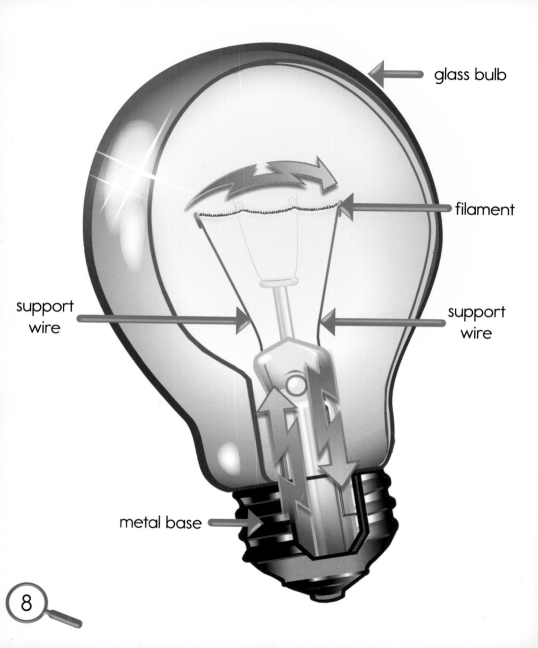

glass bulb

filament

support wire

support wire

metal base

8

How Does
It Work?

Look inside an **incandescent** (in-kan-DESS-uhnt) lightbulb. See that curly little piece of metal? It is the **filament**. When you turn on the light, electricity travels from the base of the bulb to the filament. The filament gets so hot, it glows.

So what is the glass bulb for? It keeps the filament safe. There cannot be any air inside. That would make the filament burn out. A pump sucks the air out of a lightbulb when it is being made.

This photo shows incandescent lightbulbs being made in a factory.

Still, the filament eventually burns out. The lightbulb does not work anymore. That is why we have to change lightbulbs sometimes.

Before the Bulb

Hundreds of years ago, there were no lightbulbs. Some people used candles and oil lamps for light.

Later, gaslights became popular. Gas ran through pipes into lamps in people's homes. People lit the lamps with matches. It could be pretty dangerous!

Before long, scientists began experimenting with electric bulbs.

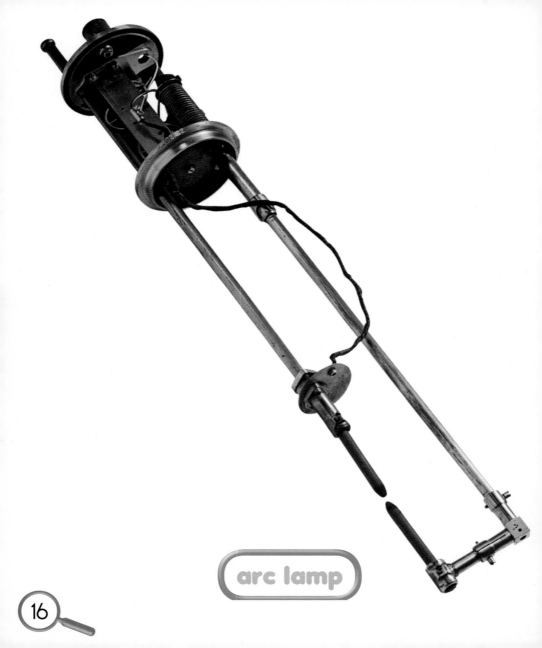

arc lamp

16

It took a long time to get the lightbulb right. The first electric light was the arc lamp. There was no filament. A spark of electricity jumped across two rods called **electrodes**.

Early incandescent bulbs did not work well. The filament broke easily.

Many people came up with different incandescent bulbs. By 1880, Thomas Edison had invented a bulb that worked for a long time. He also built a station to make electricity and send it through wires. Now people could use electric lights at home!

FUN FACT!

The bulb Edison invented had the power of 16 candles. Today's bulb gives off as much light as 150,000 candles!

Edison's
incandescent bulb

Thomas Edison in 1880

CFL stands for
Compact Fluorescent
(FLOR-es-ent) Lamp.

Different Kinds of Lightbulbs

Today there are different kinds of lightbulbs. The CFL bulb does not use a filament. It has a twisty shape and gases inside. When electricity passes into the gas, it lights up. The CFL uses less energy than an incandescent bulb. It also lasts a lot longer.

Another type of lightbulb uses LED lights. This kind of bulb uses even less energy than a CFL. It lasts longer, too.

In an LED, electricity flowing through a very tiny chip gives off light. Many small LEDs work together in a single bulb.

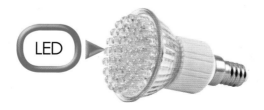

LED

These video screens in New York City use LED lights. LED stands for Light Emitting Diode (die-ODE).

Lightbulbs play such a large part in our everyday lives. We use them in reading lamps and flashlights. They light up an airport runway and so much more. It is hard to imagine a time without them!

Now you know how lightbulbs work. They make our world an even brighter place!

1879
Joseph Swan invents the first working lightbulb.

1880
Thomas Edison forms the Edison Electric Lamp Company.

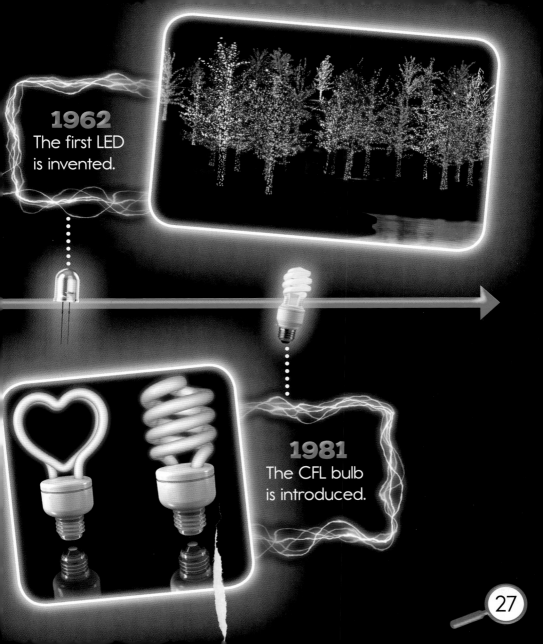

1962
The first LED
is invented.

1981
The CFL bulb
is introduced.

Ask an adult for help. Do not attempt this science experiment on your own!

When an incandescent lightbulb is screwed into a lamp, an electric current travels through wires and into the filament. The electricity makes the filament heat up. As the electricity passes through the filament, it makes the filament glow with light.

A battery can also power a lightbulb. This experiment shows you how.

You Will Need: Two 12-inch pieces of insulated copper wire, tape, D-size battery, small lightbulb (one from a flashlight will work)

1.

Ask an adult to cut away the plastic covering at both ends of the copper wires.

2.

Tape one end of one wire to the terminal at the bottom of the battery.

3.

Tape the other end of the wire to one of the lightbulb's terminals.

4.

Tape one end of the second wire to the battery's top terminal.

5.

Touch the other end of the wire to the lightbulb's other terminal. The lightbulb will light up.

Why This Works:

You have created a complete path, or a circuit. This lets the electricity flow from the battery through the lightbulb.

That's Amazing!

This photo shows what nighttime in the United States looks like from space. It was taken by NASA, the U.S. space agency. The brightest lights shine from big cities like New York, Los Angeles, and Chicago.

Glossary

electricity (i-lek-TRISS-uh-tee): form of energy that produces a charge

electrodes (i-LEK-trodes): places where electricity can move from one point to another

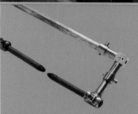

filament (FIL-uh-muhnt): thin wire that is heated by electricity to produce light

incandescent (in-kan-DESS-uhnt): glowing with light and heat

Index

Facts for Now

Visit this Scholastic Web site for more information on lightbulbs:
www.factsfornow.scholastic.com
Enter the keyword **Lightbulbs**

About the Author

Joanne Mattern is the author of many nonfiction books for children. Science is one of her favorite subjects to write about! She lives in New York State with her husband, four children, and numerous pets.